I0198650

Sandra Cruz
Collected Writings

Sandra Cruz
Collected Writings

Compiled by Markus Breitschmid
Corporis Publishers

Sandra Cruz
Collected Writings

Editor: Markus Breitschmid

© Copyright 2016
Sandra Cruz, Markus Breitschmid
All Rights Are Reserved

ISBN: 978-0-981-5553-8-6

Corporis Publishers
Zurich
Switzerland
www.corporis.ch

Printed in the United States of America

This is an anthology of writings
by Sandra Cruz I have collected.
The writings cronicle a great love.

This book is dedicated to Sandra,
the love of my life.

October 6, 2004

MY DEAR

My Dear:
In the middle of the night,
while the world is asleep,
all my thoughts turn to you...
A little star shines in my heart
and that little star is you....
There is not a place I can hide,
where I don't see you anymore...
All I can feel in these cold lonely nights
is the breath of your soul...
All I can wish is your touch,
All I can hear is your voice,
Like a fire developing under my skin...

Oh my Dear!
These lonely nights!!!
make me want your eyes,
make me wish your words!
While you are asleep,
I am dreaming of your being...

Sandra Cruz

My Dear!
If only the moon could tell you,
that I sink without you!
If only the earth could make me
gravitate towards you!
These lonely nights
turn me gray without you!

My Dear!
My sense slips away from this mundane world
to tell you that I can not live without you,
that I can not breath without your touch,
that I can not dream without you!!!
I have to scream to the entire world
that I love you so...
that I dream of your dreamy eyes
that I am only complete with you...

My Dear!
Your lips, your touch, your soul make
me want you even more in these lonely nights...
Just a little girl dreaming of you every lonely night....
Just a little girl dreaming of tomorrow,

Sandra

December 16, 2005

POETRY

What is poetry?
How can you explain?
What a wonder poetry is?

Poetry is the dance of the east
Poetry is the radiance of the west!

What is poetry?
Can I tell you in a thousand words?
Can I tell you in a million words?

Poetry is the fire
In our skin deep!

Poetry is the shining light
When darkness overtakes our sight!

Sandra Cruz

Poetry is the color in the sky
When a storm fills our soul!

Poetry is the dye in our blood
When passion claims our heart!

Poetry is the writing in the wall
When we turn blind to the moon!

For that is poetry!
Poetry in a few rods
Is touched by a God above
Comforting our lives!

Sandra Cruz

December 18, 2005

TREES

Giants of the moon!
Giants of the sun!
Giants of all there is to see
Deeply rooted in the earth!!!
Phantoms of the night...
Knights of this land!
Guarding life
All around them!
Standing still
While time goes by,
Standing still
While matter transforms!
As old as
A Star!
As tall as
The sky!
As strong as
A Knight!
Aa wise as
A king!
Mother earth has brought upon us
A wonder! A treasure!
They are made of matter!
They are made of earth!
Their rings represent
The wisdom of their skin!

Sandra Cruz

Their branches reach out
To all which has a soul!
Their leaves present us
With a rainbow of light!
Their eternal presence
Comforts our sight!
The wind blows over them!
And they sing a song!!
A song of life!
A song of war!
A song of peace!
A song of joy!
They chant about
Forgotten heroes!
They chant about
Forgotten places!
They chant days!!!
There... They are....
Standing still below the rain!
Crying without tears
For what they have witnessed!
Crying for you and I!
Crying for all that is alive!!!!

Sandra Cruz

14

February 17, 2006

TIME

Treacherous over joy palpitating
Within the branches of a heart...
Unknown sentiment to the fate
Of a rotten corpse!

Blazing wings overcrowding
An eternal sky....
Streets made of blood
Dripping over each single stone....

Time has brought upon us
A deceiving destiny!

Can we dare to claim a voice for us?
Can we dare to claim an instant of life?

Emptiness awaits the ignorance
Of my fellow mortals!

Time holds all the keys!
Time owns all the doors!
Time possesses all the locks!

Indignity lays a cloud over
An unedifying dying flower!

Here, we are...

Sandra Cruz

Praying to exist!
Praying to live!
Praying to be!

Supplicating an unknown being
For a time that doesn't exist!
For a time that murderers our souls!

Here, we are...

Hoping for a light that
Has never been lit!
Hoping for a tomorrow
That will never be born!

Oh....miserable souls!

Endless ignorance surrounds your struggle!
Endless despair claims your will!
Endless pain infiltrates your breath!

Oh....miserable souls!

Knowing that a carcass,
Your flesh will become!
Knowing that time
Will destroy all your cells!

Oh...miserable souls!

16

Begging for a miracle
Without a God!

Imploring for a vision
Without a cause!

Pleading for a time
Without an end!

Urging for a life
That is already gone!

Oh...miserable souls!

Tears in the skull
Fill the awaiting space!
Sorrow has made
A scar into every turn!

A superimposing space,
Creates can not escape,
Has already proclaimed
Our time,
Our hope,
Our life!

Sandra Cruz

February 26, 2006

OLYMPICS

Lights above shining
Thru everyone's sight

Passion leading the way
To the infinite milky way...

Hope rushing
Thru everyone's pulse

Flames lining the instant
Of an infinite sky...

The world coming to a pause
To witness a bloody battle...

A ruthless fight
Among the greatest...

Speed overtaking a simple
Body of matter..

Sweat possessing
Every pore in the skin...

Crossing a line
Takes over a life...

Crossing a line
Takes over a hope...

Crossing a line
Takes over every single breath!

Crossing a line
Takes over an instant of glory...

Racing to be he first
And win the golden reward...

All united as one...

For an everlasting love,
For the love of the game...
For the love of being best...

For the love of the fire
Within every soul!

For the love of a heart
Palpitating as one...

For the love of humankind!!!

Sandra Cruz

April 28, 2006

TIME

The time for you and I is gone...
The time for us is history...
The time, my darling, has flown away...
A faceless man stands before me now...

Our time has passed...
Our beginning has ended and
Our end has become certainty...

Time to reflect...
I will always be yours...as
Much as you can claim...

I can only understand if you
Want to walk away...
My time with you burnt our love...
What can I say?
The instances of my humanity
Had become a barrier between you and I, my darling...

My time is gone now...
And all I can do is stand up and
Keep tucked away in my heart
The images of your smile...

I wish you luck in your new ventures...
I wish you....love, above all things...

Sandra

August 11 2006

DUALITY

I am dual...
I am one but dual...
Dual to the rigors of the world!
Within my stratum...
Two different images subsist...
One empathizes with the social order...
One adulates thoughts...

I am dual...
Traveling to the limbo of my funeral!
Walking towards mundanity...
Eclipsing the solar system...
Emerging into an apparatus of corruption...

I am dual...
Dying of thirst for ecstasy...
Gasping for any instance of wisdom...
Breeding countless ideas..
Searching for sensual bliss...

I am dual... and I am the one...

I am the one...
Imploring for a revelation
In the midst of my sleep...

I am the one..
Desperately waiting for
God's stroke!

Sandra Cruz

I am the one
Bathing under the stars
Of my own obsessions...

I am the one...
Cremating those alive...
To the sight of my words!

I am the one...
I am... I am...

I am the one...
Seeking life while
Writing of the dead...

I am the one...
Seeking pleasure in
The suffering of my two worlds!

I am the one...
Deceitful to men
About my mundane being!

I am the one...
Frigid entertaining
A meaningless space!

I am the one...
Becoming alive solely by
Dreaming, thinking
Suffering, loving...

I am the one...
Agonizing over my duality
While confronting my demons...

I am the one...
Enjoying the pleasures of
My spirituality while
Closing my ears to the commoners...

I am the one... and I am dual!
I am a lie and
I am the truth!
I am the way and
I am the end!
I am a role and
I am a soul!
I am dead and
I am alive!

I am dual...
A character whisking away...
My individuality!
A soul nourishing...
My freedom!

I am! I am !
I am the one and I am dual

Sandra Cruz

December 18, 2006

MY DEAR

My Dear!
In tender nights like this...
When the sky is empty
And stars are faulty,
I dream of your eyes
Guiding this soul of mine!

My Dear!
As far as I can see
And as long as I can feel,
Your breath proclaims
This aged body of mine!

My Dear!
Tonight the sky is young...
And lovers dance in the moon!

My Dear!
The night merciless
Steals your shadow
From the glitter above!

My Dear!
Whispers in the clouds
Can be hear in the
Streams of my silence!

My Dear!
My words are empty tonight
A cascade of notes
Invades my ears!

My Dear!
My passion grows as
Each sound touches
The darkness of my sight!

My Dear!
Loneliness acquires a
New meaning in this
Fantasy world!

My Dear!
The pain of your absence
Makes me feel alive!

My Dear!
Your touch makes me
Feel human!

My Dear!
Words of hope
Rest over my body!

Sandra Cruz

My Dear!
It is too late to be
Hopeful

My Dear!
Dead came upon me
At this hour!

My Dear!
Death took the pain
Away from my skin

My Dear!
Thanks to this earthly
Body of mine,
I can finally say:
Good night!

Good night! My Dear!
I am holding your hand
As I depart ...My Dear!
I am resting in peace now...
Good night! My Dear!

Sandra Cruz

September 25, 2007

Dear Markus:

I feel overwhelmed that you want to do a
painting of me...Just don't tell anyone is supposed
to be me!!! I would be very embarrassed...:) Just
because I am shy...Nothing to do with you...
I like all of them...You are the artist so you should
pick...and I know that it will probably won't look like
me at the end....

Sandra

Sandra Cruz

Undated

THE DECLINE

Ancient empires
Crumbling into the deep-sea ...

Lines of lineage
Decaying into dust ...

Foundations of stone
Vanishing into the air ...

Palpable ignorance is burying away ...
The past! The present! The future!
The history of the world!
The greatness of the human race!

Melting away into rubble....
The craft of magicians is!

Rings of commodity greedily devour ...
The artful longevity of creation!

Obscure dimensions have become...
The center of gravity!
The axis of existence!

Corrosive unshapely matter
Rules the desires of the flesh!

Sandra Cruz

The mind is dead!
The body is hollow!

For only a soulless body stands!
Without meaning, without ardor,
Devoid of a touch by God!!

Senseless bodies without flair
Possess our earth!

What has become of our minds?
What has become of our humanity?

Still life menaces...
The sumptuousness of the moon!
The warmness of the sun!
The vastness of the sky!

Tears of sorrow have become...
The constant companion
Of those searching for a muse!

The fire is left behind
For minds become corpses of the soil...
For monstrosity overshadows
The fainted vision of the hear....

The mind is dead!
The body is hallow!

The curtains are down...
The windows are closed...
The doors are locked...
The spirit deceased...

And a long overdue
"Farewell" of our earthiness
Becomes the single certainty
Of our broken existence
Of our departed soul!!!

Sandra

Sandra Cruz

Undated

MY DEAR MARKUS

I keep tucked away in my heart
The images of your smile.....

Your voice has become an
Endless song in my ears...

Your smell surrounds the
Infinity of my lonely nights...

Your shadow merciless
Saturates my vision...

In endless days like this,
The pain of our absence
Makes me feel alive...

In endless days like this,
Restless hope
Has become my faithful companion...

In endless days like this
Melancholy outshines
The phantoms residing in
My mind...

In endless days like this,
The memories of you and me
Have become my heaven....

Sandra

March 6, 2008

ETERNITY

One question remains in the endless of times....
As the day vanishes under the scrutiny of the skies...
The night emerges as a hasty rage of grayness...
Sovereign it conquers unattainable frontiers!

The clear yet mysterious sights above proclaim
The intensity of the ones below.....
Under a blanket of uncertainty...
The ones beneath question:
The meaning of the being....
Yet ... Answers to prayers... None exist!
Only the coldness of the dark arrives and
Overtakes the soulless men under their spell....

Are they joyful now?
Certainly! They are!
For they know nothing,
other than their dull souls...
And life goes by and goes by
Without sentiment for the spirits....
The bliss that once proclaimed the universe
is forbidden from this earth!

A sudden stillness entangles their bare minds....
And their minds are diminished by unwritten thoughts....
But are they genuine thoughts?
Are those the ones that intensity existence?
Are those thoughts the ones that full fill the
inquisitiveness of our temper?

Sandra Cruz

Are those the ones that bring calmness to our being?
Are those the ones that arduously arise our passion?

And the same inquiry remains under the same
darkness of time!!!!
What prophecy could answer our doubts?
What organ could hear our prayers?
What soul could deliver our ecstasy?
What sound could lift our spirits?

All the erroneous places are under scrutiny!!!
We are searching for the light in the darkness space...
We are searching for tomorrow in the days long gone....
We are searching for answers in the mistaken cells!

The answers were already within us....
The answers were already in the path we took....
The answers were already inside our flesh....
The answers were already in our own self...

There ...they were!
Only a few ones could see beyond their times....
Only a few ones could see above their earth...
Only a few ones could see past their own existence...
Only a few ones arrived triumphal
to the no ending times!!!!

Sandra

34

Undated

INERTIA

Inertia succumbs the alter ego
Of my fellows....

Larvas growth and multiply
Into the masses of reason...

Feeding off putrid blood...
Feeding off toxic air...
Feeding off fatal consent...

Lethargic governs
The existence of any sign of life....

Infestation of degradation
Runs thru their veins....

Conformity in convention generates
A useless breed...
A worthless race...

Like cannibals
Searching for an instant gratification...

Sandra Cruz

Disregarding:
The joy of the mind...
The joy of the earth...
The joy of life...

Indifference has become one with
These dull creatures....

Deprivation of ecstasy...
A magnificent prize!
For the tolerance of being alive...

Standing still thru time...
Waiting to exhale...

Accomplishing horrifying acts...
Destroying every cell...
Exterminating every wing...
Killing every flame...
Wiping out any hope....

Merciless creatures to their
Own existence...

Ruthless condemn to apathy
Each instant of breathable air...

Being? Living? Thinking?
What for!!!
Survival becomes their aim...
Numbness reign their brains...

Cold-blooded creatures
Achieving rapid extinction...

Extinction of ideas...
Extinction of dreams...
Extinction of creation...
Extinction of time....

Inert, they have become!
Inert to the true meaning of
Being alive!!!

Sandra Cruz

August 1, 2008

A Loving Note:

Markus, I just wanted to share some words with you. I don't know if you remember this e-mail but you wrote those words to me and I am very glad you did. I don't know if you still feel the same way as you did when you wrote this message. I can only share with you how I feel and what I sense about us.

I am still 'crazy' about you. As crazy as I was 7+ years ago and even more now that time has passed. I feel deeply that we have a strong 'love connection, in all senses of that word. I believe that time can only weaken relationships that are somewhat fragile to begin with. Time has passed and the love I have for you gets stronger and more intense than before. Time only reassures me that our relationship is strong, solid, intense, and full of passion. After such a long time together, I still feel 'sparks' and pleasure when I am with you. I believe that you also feel something like that because I can sense it. The times with you are always something I look forward.

I believe that we are very much attracted to each other after all these years. I believe that we turn each other on and that we have similar ideas and needs about sex. When I think about all of the years together, I find it unbelievable that we are still so 'turn on' by each other. I think that's a good sign in a relationship because sexual chemistry plays a significant role in keeping a relationship alive. Otherwise, everything becomes dull and unsatisfactory. I do acknowledge that the intensity of our sex life changes sporadically from time to time but I believe that is normal. What is important is how intensely sexually attracted we are to each other even after so many years. I like that we share our ideas about sex and sexual fantasies and that we are compatible in what turns us on. We like to have sex and explore ways to intensify our sex life. I never mentioned anything but this is important to me since I always have all of these fantasies in my head but I am scare to share them with anyone else other than you. I want to continue to explore.. I know that at this point, I want to take things further up and go to another place/level as intensely as I believe you want it too. I want to make all of our fantasies a reality.

I think we have a very good relationship. We have constructed a relationship based on chemistry, love, care, intimacy and trust. I have never been so intimate with anyone as I am with you. I feel so comfortable with you...you cannot imagine. I feel free to do or say anything and to share my deepest thoughts. Our relationship feels very good. It feels like it is something real, something genuine and even magical. I think that you also know that. The relationship I have with you is very important in my life.

We have fun together, we like each other, we are sexually attracted to each other, and we enjoy similar things. I think we are extremely compatible even thought I also know that we are different. But I also think different is good in a way otherwise it would be so boring two people that are so similar to each other.

I love you very much and I am very much in love with you. The spark has never been so intense and the passion can only grow. As far as I can sense, my whole

Sandra Cruz

being desires you and I. I can only hope or dream that you feel the same way. "Us" for me feels so good, so right and so joyful that time only becomes a yearning of the body and the heart. Time only gives me space to whisper in the clouds that this body of mine is yours and that every moment/second/day/month/year seeks your presence in my life.

I want you to know how I feel and I hope these feeling are reciprocal. I want to be in your life but only if you want it too. I will understand if you want something else and I will never become an obstacle in your life. If someone else makes you happy and fulfills you then no one can change that. If another person can damage our relationship then our relationship is not fulfilling anymore anyways. I hope that you know what you want. I know that I will missed you terribly and feel that part of me is gone if you were not longer in my life.

One day you asked me to answer this question before, is my life better with Markus or without Markus? The answer is my life is better with Markus. Ask yourself the same question. Is your life better with Sandra or without Sandra?

I will always love you and I will always be thankful for the time spend together,

Sandra

August 13, 2008

My adored Markus:

My spirit yearns your touch from this
Place in the universe where only
written words can reach you...

Every step of the way, your vision becomes
The inspiration rooted in my cells...
The madness embedded in my dreams...
The music that elevates my spirit...

Dreaming of times gone by,
My spirit is filled with melancholic thoughts
For I long your presence in my life.

When I open my eyes, I must sight
For a higher revelation than all wisdom,
It is the flesh of your bones that
Intoxicates me with ardor...

My adore Markus,

I am the one here waiting for you,
I am the one dreaming of your touch...
I am the one hoping for a tomorrow....
I am the one toasting for the memories
Of you and I...

Yesterday, today and tomorrow...
I will love you until the end of my times...

Love,
Sandra

Sandra Cruz

March 1, 2009

BABY NAMES

Camille	unisex	servant for the temple
Christopher	male	he who Christ in his heart
Cruz	male	cross
Emmanuel	male	god is with us
Grabiele	male	god is my strength
Isabel	female	
Ludwig	male	famous fighter
Massimiliano	male	greatest
Massimo	male	greatest
Maximiliamo	male	greatest
Salvatore	male	savior
Stephano	male	victorious
Vittorious	male	conqueror

March 8, 2009

Dear Markus:

I hope your last few days in Beijing are good. I just wanted to write a few words to tell you how much I love you.. Lately, I have been thinking a lot about what the future entails. While I am excited to continue pursing my dreams and goals , I also think of you. A few days ago, I thought nothing else will make me happier than to to live in an urban place, having a good job and living my own life. I always wanted to live life my way... to dream, to cry, to struggle, to be happy, to achieve things own my own....
That's just part of who I am... I do not want to feel confine to a space to a life that I do not want... and while the thought of this makes me happy... I can not bear the thought of living without you....
This interview on Monday has made me happy but it has also open my eyes to confront what the future holds... The thought of being away from you tears my heart into pieces and the happiness that I am supposed to feel vanishes when I think of my life without you....

Sandra Cruz

Markus, you are everything to me... my yesterday, my today, my tomorrow, my forever...
I love you more than you can ever dream of...
While I think of the future, I can not imagine one without you..
While my dreams steer me towards an unknown space, I can not bear the thought of a space without you...
I do not know what the future holds... I do not have answers for my doubts...
All I wanted to share with you is that in my heart there is only one name... and that name is your name...
I do not know where I will be in a few years but I wanted to tell you that you will always be part of me....
For who I am is because of you....
For who I am can not be without you any longer...
For who I am is what my heart wants... you!

I hope this is not too corny or cheesy...
I wrote a little something to commemorate our "8 years together"... ODE TO OUR FIRST ENCOUNTER
I am attaching it.. It is dedicated to you...
I hope you like....if you can understand it...lol

Love,

Sandra

44

March 8, 2009

ODE TO THE FIRST ENCOUNTER

An unforeseen revelation
Came to my being to
Unlock the secrecy of my inner self...

Under the depth ness of the sky...
Under the unlikeness of premonitions...
Under the pretense of commonalty.

Your soul aroused from the shadows...
captivating my sight...
conquering my existence.

One glance...One word....
One touch... One kiss...
One heart... One you...

Earth stood still
Below the frantic call of times
Proclaiming your silence...

Life vividly began
From the ashes of the soil
To the lightness of being...

Senses aroused as
A cascade of a thousand pulses
beneath the skin of my flesh...

Sandra Cruz

Clamors became unheard
Under the magical vision
Of your blue eyes...

And as times devours my tissues...
Your smell is embedded in my cells...
Your warm is fuel to my muscles ...

Every year is suspended in the
Perpetuity of space because of
the miraculous certainty of your existence.

One answer to all questions still remains
after so many years:
I am because you are!

Eternally yours,
Sandra

April 8, 2010

FOREVER AND EVER

Dear Markus:

Time comes around and solely one question seems
to capture your wondering of your life with me.... One
question keeps surrounding your rationality.... I do
too have the same question gravitating towards my
rationality.... I do too wonder what it is that life wants
out of me...I do too wonder if life is to be living the way
we want it. So, a few words about my humanity....

Loneliness captures my heart and blinds my feelings....
Sometimes, sadness becomes the domain
of my existence...
The feeling of helplessness becomes one
with my brain...
Nothingness takes possession of my reality....

But once you walk into my room, into my life...
Death does not exist anymore....
The pain in my heart does not hurt anymore...

You give me life....
You resuscitate me from my darkest hours....
You lay next to me and my deepest sorrow disappears...

I am trying to conquer the world but
The world turns out to be you... and only you....
You give me the courage to live...

You give the strength to pursue my freedom....
You give me wings when I was born in chains...

Sandra Cruz

The air is cleaner...
The colors are brighter...
The dreams are joyful....
The existence is full of substance
 And is all due to you!

Oh, my Markus....
What should I call you?
My oxygen? My blood? My music?
My hero? My dream? My all?
What adjective could even encapsulate YOU?

As years go by, my love grows and grows even deeper
and deeper....
My hair is turning gray...
My skin begins to sag....
My bones become weaker...
And wrinkles appear in my face....

But only one certainty remains...
That the best of my life is you...
So I will always remain...
A woman whose heart belongs to one being...
And one being only...forever and ever.... or until I cease
to exist...

Sandra

48

September 13, 2011

A LIFE LESS ORDINARY

Here I am....
Counting years as they pass thru the absoluteness of
space...
Here I am....Thirty four years old...
An age defined by the imagination of my species ....
...the human kind...

Here I am....
Lifeless
Childless
Loveless....

Emptiness arises in every turn taken...
Voices murmur sounds that are incomprehensible....
Space filled with nothingness overtakes my soul...

Here I am...
Dreamless
Hopeless
Motionless...

The demands of my own inert existence,
Beg my senses for a heartbeat...
Plead for a sign of consciousness...

Sandra Cruz

But I am still here...
Laying motionless to the sound of your voice...
Unmoved by your touch...
Unresponsive to you and me....

This corpse can not shed more tears...
Yesterday is gone...
Today is uncertain ...
Tomorrow does not exist...

Here I am...
Begging for a sign...
Imploring for commotion...
Praying for a life less ordinary....

Sandra

September 16, 2011

EL PASO DEL TIEMPO

La vida es para vivirla sin costos ni beneficios...
El paso del tiempo solo corresponse a un momento
imaginario...
El reloj hace tick tack....
y ese sonido tan grotesco...
llena el ser con un deseo intangible de correr contra
los propios deseos...

Aqui estoy sentanda...
Esclavizada por los segudos de
Un tiempo inventado por la imaginacion....

El paso del tiempo solo
Se apodera de las ganas de vivir
Y al final solamente crecen las dudas,
Las pregunats, los adioses...

Quien se ha inventado esta idea tan grotesca?
Acaso ha sido ese Dios inventado por las religions?
Acaso ha sido la humanidad, anhelando una verdad
que no existe?
O acaso he sido yo, el mas humilde de todos los
servidores?

El paso del tiempo es tan fugaz como un respire...
Como el anhelo de vivir para siempre...
Como un deseo carnal que pasa y se extingue...

Sandra Cruz

September 16, 2011

QUOTES

To die,
What is to die other than to cease feeling?
What is to die other than to stop breathing?
What is to die other than to return to the place where
we came from?

The heart wants what the heart wants....but the brain...
Oh! The brain always complicates matters!

Death only means that the soul can finally rest in
peace

Time suffocates the desire for existence

Love releases endorphins but enslaves the freedom to
be, but then again...
what is a high without a low! What is a yesterday
without a today?

What is poetry other than a shinning light when
darkness overtakes it all?

Poetry is the dye in our blood when fever claims our
brains!

Life is to be lived without cost or benefits

History is told by those who write it

January 19, 2012

A BREATH OF AIR FILLS MY LUNGS WITH OXYGEN

A breath of air fills my lungs with oxygen
And my heart grows and grows to
Uncover that I am still alive....

The corporal world screams at my brain:
You are alive, you are alive...
The muscles are moving!
the eyes are blinking!
The ears are listening!
Then, it must be: I am alive....

The senses perceive the natural world...
Everything tells me I am alive...
But what is truly to be alive?

Sandra Cruz

Valentine's Day - February 14, 2012

Dear Markus:

I am happy to spend another year together. I hope that the rest of my years are with you. You are the one who makes my heart beat faster and fills my existence with joy and hope!

So, I am giving you my heart as a sign of the eternal love I feel for you!

Your loving wife,
Sandra

March 15, 2012

AS THE DAY DISAPPEARS
UNDER THE SCRUTINY OF THE SKIES

As the day disappears under the scrutiny of the skies....
One question remains in the darkness of time.....
The night appears as a sudden rage of unequilibrium
and reaches frontiers that could have never be thought
of....
The clear yet mysterious sights above proclaim
The intensity of the ones below.....
Under a blanket of uncertainty.....
The ones below question:
The meaning of the being....
Answers to prayers... None exist....
Only the coldness of the dark arrives and
Overtakes the soulless men under their spell....

Are they joyful now?
Certainly! they are ! for they know nothing other than
mundane needs of their
Simply souls...
And life goes by and goes by without sentiment for the
spirits....
The bliss that once proclaimed the universe is
forbidden from earth....
A sudden warm deepest inside their minds....
And the mind is diminish by unwritten thoughts....
But are they genuine thoughts?
Are those the ones that intensify existence?
Are those thoughts the ones that full fill the
inquisitiveness of our temper?

Sandra Cruz

Are those the ones that bring calmness to our
existence?

And the same inquiry remains under the same
darkness of time!!!!
What a prophecy could answer our doubts!
What a voice could hear our prayers!
What s soul could deliver fullness.....

All the wrong places are under scrutiny!!!
We are searching for the light in the darkness room.....
We are searching for tomorrow in the past....
We are searching for answers in the mistaken cells!

The answers were already inside us....
The answers were already in the path we took....
The answers were already within our skin.....
The answers were in the shining eyes of our own
reflection....

There ...they were....and only a few ones could see
beyond their time....
Only a few ones could see above their earth...
Only a few ones could see above their own
existence!!!!
Only a few ones arrived triumphal to the no ending
times!!!!

Sandra

56

April 24, 2012

THE IMPORTANCE OF BEING

One is born ...
One lives...
Then one dies....

Born
One can only be one and never two or three or more...
For one is only born one and thus one should always
remain one...

We come to be alone
We are born free of the attachments of
This world... Thus, we are born to be free...

Lives...
One lives and one can only live life in
His/her own terms...
And no one else's terms
Because life is meant to be lived once and only once...

Sandra Cruz

Death....
We are born to die...
For we are meant to return to the place
Where we came from...
For life does not come to be
Without the grand finale of death!

What is a life without a grandiose beginning?

What is life without a series of experiences?

What is life without a dramatic ending?

Sandra Cruz

"Everything will be alright in the end. If it is not alright, then, it is not yet the end."

May 7, 2012

THE LAST WORDS I WROTE TO YOU

It was a breezy Sunday...
Alone deeply emerged in my thoughts...
Scarce memories of you and I....
Haunting my senses...

My stubborn heart
Longing a word.. a sign...
Imagining your smile,
The color of you eyes.
 your smell!

Then, my hands wanted to speak
And wrote to you...
Those very last words without
Knowing that those words were the last words
I were to write to you....

Sandra Cruz

Those few words were the last words
Of the reminiscent of you and I
Those words were the end of our story...
Those words will continue to cry
Until I have the courage to shed tears!

The last few words I wrote to you were:

"Have I mentioned the three things I have
done today so far?
I miss you, I miss you, and I miss you"

And those words marked the end of you and I!

Sandra

November 7, 2012

A PLEDGE TO HUMANITY

Must it be? It must be!
We have a president!
Someone said, "God bleeds America now"...
Does it?
Once again united as one humankind
We elected the path of hope....
Even as divided as we are by our genetic make-up
We elected to keep walking out of the darkness
The emotional sentiments are all the same...
Our joint voices were firm and strong...
And those voices were heard!
A pledge for a better system...
A pledge for a better reality...
A pledge for better times...
A case for Humanity...
Where reason enlightens
The possibilities of a fair and just government...
A government of the people, by the people, for the
people...

Sandra Cruz

Does God bleed America now?
Perhaps it does...Perhaps it does not...
But we are still here...
Full of dreams, full of hopes, full of life...
Yesterday is history,
Today is now,
Tomorrow is yet to be.
But we are still here....
And as long as we are still here,
There would always be hope.

Sandra Cruz

After my Last Visit to You - November 8, 2012

CARIOT

Would you write to me when I am gone?
Would you remember my face?
Would you remember my smell?
Would you remember my name?

My darling...
I will remember your name...
I will remember your face...
I will remember your smell...

Here I am..thinking of you...
Of your whole being....
Of you and I...
Of our times together....

A tear comes down my face...
And I turn around...
Looking for your being....
But you are already gone...

My darling...
You are gone
and so I am ...

What happened to you and I?
What happened to our time?
What happened to us?

Sandra Cruz

My darling...
I will always cry when
I remember us...
I will always cry silently...
Remembering you...

Why does it hurt so bad?
Why is the sand so infinite?
Why is the sky so blue?
Why are you gone?

My darling,
I will keep walking...
I will keep breathing...
I will keep living...

But now you are part of my
My skin.....
For good or bad....

You are part of my existence...
For now, for tomorrow and for forever....

My darling....

Sandra

October 21, 2014

WHATEVER HAPPENED TO THAT GIRL

Whatever happened to the girl?
That was sitting on the roof...
Waiting to growth wings to fly...

What ever happened to the girl?
That used to devour every single book
She found...

What ever happened to the girl?
Daydreaming of the world...
Imagining giants made of shadows ...

Whatever happened to that girl?
Who wanted to explore ancient worlds..
Ancient lives...

Whatever happened to that girl?
That dreamt of unspoken languages
Unspoken dreams...

Whatever happened to that girl?
Who saw rainbows even
In the darkest hours...

Whatever happened to that girl?
Who wanted to conquer life...
Even in the most lifeless place...

Sandra Cruz

Whatever happened to you?
Did you fall asleep?

Did you go numb to the wonders of the world?
Did you died?
Are you still there?

Whatever happened to you?
Did you lose all senses for life?
Did you become desensitized to those around you?
Did you become one more...
One more of the soulless souls?

Whatever happened to you spirit?
To you thirst for life?
To the imagination that once ruled mind?

Is it all gone?
Did you become one more?
One more of all there is to be known....
One more of a lifeless existence....
Or is your heart still beating?

Sandra

October 23, 2014

DISEASE

Disease corrodes your body
Bit by bit takes possession of your strength
Bit by bit takes over your hope

The declining of your body
Emcompasses the decline of your mind...

Sandra Cruz

68

The first time I saw Sandra was in the cafeteria of the University of North Carolina in Charlotte, North Carolina in February 2001. Shortly thereafter we were a couple.

We got married in a civil ceremony in Christiansburg, Virginia on May 15, 2010 and in a Roman-Catholic ceremony at the Jesuit Church in Lucerne, Switzerland on August 3, 2010. I was never more happy and content in my life than as I was then.

Sandra left on July 7, 2012. Our marriage was disolved on March 22, 2016. The sadness endures.

No one has loved me as Sandra did nor can I imagine I ever will love someone the way I love Sandra.
Sandra is the love of my life.

www.ingramcontent.com/pod-product-compliance
Lightning Source LLC
Chambersburg PA
CBHW070831100426
42813CB00003B/574

9 780981 555386